629.4
Cas

Casanellas, Antonio
Great discoveries & . . .
earth . . .

LINDOP SCHOOL
2400 S. 18TH AVENUE
BROADVIEW, IL 60155

NO QUIZ

Edmund F Lindop School
2400 South 18th Avenue
Broadview, Illinois 60155-3974

DEMCO

That Helped Explore
Earth and Space

For a free color catalog describing Gareth Stevens Publishing's list of high-quality books and multimedia programs, call 1-800-542-2595 (USA) or 1-800-461-9120 (Canada). Gareth Stevens Publishing's Fax: (414) 332-3567.

The editor would like to extend thanks to Randy Farchmin, science instructor, Milwaukee Area Technical College, Milwaukee, Wisconsin, for his kind and professional help with the information in this book.

Library of Congress Cataloging-in-Publication Data

Casanellas, Antonio.
 [Tierra y el espacio. English]
 Great discoveries and inventions that helped explore earth and space / by Antonio Casanellas; illustrated by Ali Garousi.
 p. cm. — (Great discoveries and inventions)
 Includes bibliographical references and index.
 Summary: Explains how early inventions, including those of the sundial and compass, as well as more recent discoveries, have helped scientists explore outer space; includes science experiments relating to these instruments.
 ISBN 0-8368-2584-5 (lib. bdg.)
 1. Astronautics—Juvenile literature. 2. Outer Space—Exploration—Juvenile literature. [1. Astronautics. 2. Outer Space—Exploration.]
I. Garousi, Ali, ill. II. Title. III. Series.
TL793.C37 2000
629.4—dc21   99-053262

First published in North America in 2000 by
Gareth Stevens Publishing
A World Almanac Education Group Company
330 West Olive Street, Suite 100
Milwaukee, WI 53212 USA

This U.S. edition © 2000 by Gareth Stevens, Inc. Original edition © 1999 by Ediciones Lema, S.L., Barcelona, Spain. Translated from the Spanish by Flor de Lis Igualada. Photographic composition and photo mechanics: Novasis, S.A.L., Barcelona (Spain). Additional end matter © 2000 by Gareth Stevens, Inc.

Printed in the United States of America

1 2 3 4 5 6 7 8 9 04 03 02 01 00

Gareth Stevens Publishing
A WORLD ALMANAC EDUCATION GROUP COMPANY

The Heliograph

Earth has a twenty-four hour day because of the way it spins while orbiting the Sun. Since ancient times, humans have created methods of measuring time so that they could plan their days. The invention of the sundial allowed people to do just this. The heliograph is a modern-day version of the sundial. This instrument, also called the Campbell-Stokes sunshine recorder, is used worldwide at weather stations to measure the total number of sunshine hours per day. A glass ball stands in a curved base that is lined with a strip of sun-sensitive paper. The ball acts as a large magnifying glass and concentrates the rays of the Sun onto the paper. As the Sun moves across the sky, it burns a mark on the paper. Each night, the paper is removed and is replaced with new paper. The hours of sunlight can be calculated simply by studying the strips of paper. Modern versions use photocells.

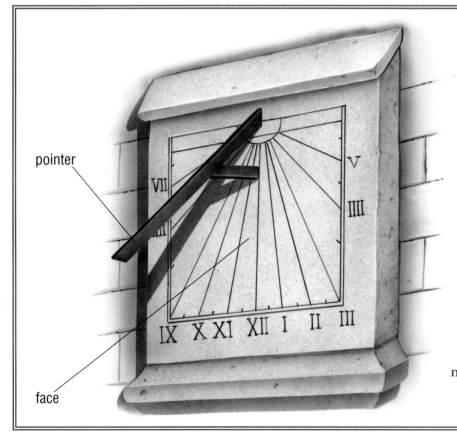

pointer

face

HOW A SUNDIAL WORKS

Sundials were the clocks and heliographs of the past. The face of a sundial is marked with the hours of the day. A pointer is positioned on the sundial in such a way that when the Sun shines down onto the sundial, its shadow points to the time of day. A sundial's face can be positioned upright, like this one *(left)* built into a wall, or it can be level with the flat horizon. A sundial can also be made to stand alone. Today, sundials are made for decoration, although they still tell the solar time.

HORIZONTAL SUNDIAL

This was another type of clock. The time was indicated by the length of the shadow.

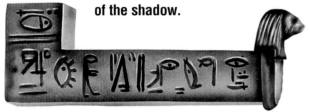

pointer

SEASONAL CHANGES

This sundial *(right)* had two interchangeable pointers. One was used in summer and the other in winter.

sun-sensitive paper

glass ball

CHARTING SUNSHINE

The Campbell-Stokes sunshine recorder *(left)* is a modern version of old sundials. Weather stations use it to measure how many hours of sunlight there are in each day. Recent versions use photocells.

sample of marked paper

Space Probes

Galileo Galilei was the first to use telescopes to make a scientific study of the night sky. He made important discoveries that helped him understand the universe and, in particular, our own solar system. Astronomy has advanced a lot since then, and in recent years, the world's wealthier countries have launched space probes in order to study the other planets of the solar system. Scientists calculate exact flight paths for the space probes and program them to travel close enough to some planets that they can take photographs of them. Some of these probes have actually landed on the planets nearest to Earth and have analyzed their soil and atmosphere, or air. For example, the space probe *Viking* was transported by an orbiter spacecraft, which descended over Mars. The lander successfully touched down on the planet's surface. This was possible due to the lander's parachute and its special folding legs, which absorbed the shock of the fall.

THE MOVEMENT OF SOLAR SYSTEM PLANETS

In 1543, Nicolaus Copernicus published his theory that the planets revolve around the Sun and that Earth is one of the planets. This theory is called heliocentric, or Sun-centered. Galileo, in the early seventeenth century, used telescopes to study the planets. He found that Venus goes through phases from new to full, just as our Moon does as it circles Earth. Mercury also has phases. Phases occur when, from our view on Earth, changing areas of a planet receive sunlight. These observations *(right)* proved Copernicus's heliocentric theory — the Sun did not revolve around Earth. Today, space probes add to our knowledge of the planets.

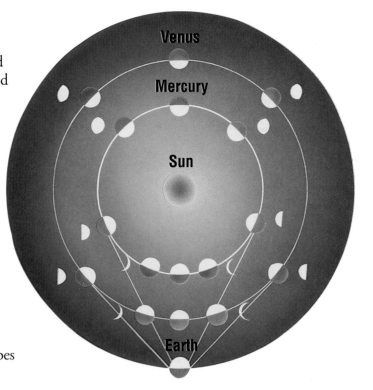

THE SPACE PROBE *VIKING*

Two space probes of this type were sent to Mars and were able to land on the planet's surface. They collected ground samples and took several photographs. The journey to Mars took a whole year!

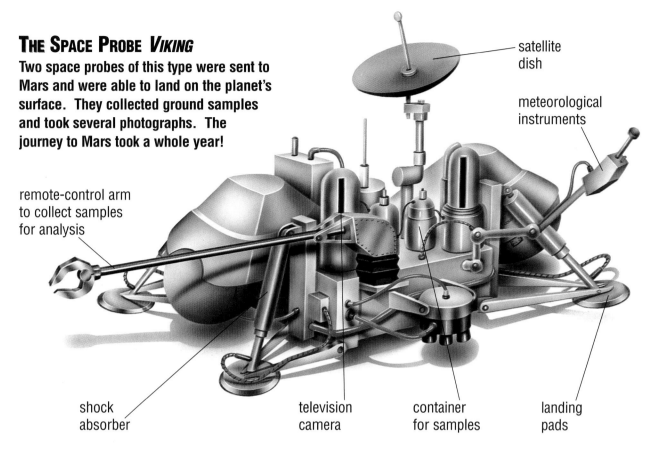

satellite dish

meteorological instruments

remote-control arm to collect samples for analysis

shock absorber

television camera

container for samples

landing pads

PROBING OUTER PLANETS

To study the planets farthest from Earth, two probes of this type *(below)* were launched into space. *Voyager 1* and *2* traveled close enough to the outer planets to take photographs.

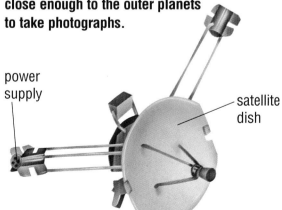

power supply

satellite dish

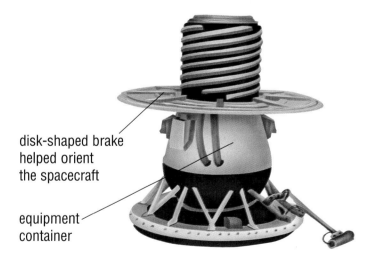

disk-shaped brake helped orient the spacecraft

equipment container

VENUS PROBE

The Russian spaceship *Venera 9 (above)* landed on Venus. It filmed the surface and sent the images back to Earth.

Space Stations

Recent technological developments have improved current machines and made possible the creation of several new ones. One of the major driving factors of these improvements has been space exploration, which has speeded up scientific discoveries in fields like communications, electronics, and the characteristics of materials. One of the most recent projects is the creation of space stations.

In these stations, the construction of certain objects would be much easier. On Earth, it is difficult to manufacture some objects, such as bearings and steel foam, which can be made only inside a vacuum. They could be made in space factories, housing up to four hundred people. The large outside cylinders shown in the illustration below would rotate to provide a feeling of gravity.

LIVING IN SPACE

Space stations of the future would need a regular transport system to bring supplies to the people on the station.

ROBOTICS

Space discoveries have been made possible by the huge developments in robotics. Robots are machines that can be programmed to perform tasks that, up until now, only a human has been able to do. They are controlled by computers whose instructions direct the robots' tasks. The computer transmits an order to the moving parts, which then perform that particular operation. Most robot actions are performed by a large arm, like the one shown in this illustration. The development of robotics for space programs has led to industrial and manufacturing uses that have dramatically increased the speed of production.

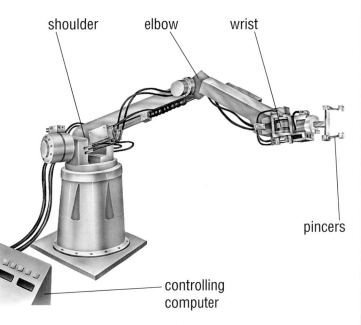

shoulder   elbow   wrist

pincers

controlling computer

SPACE SICKNESS

Zero gravity in space causes a shift of fluid to the upper part of the body. People then experience headaches, dizziness, and nausea, among other effects. Loss of muscle and of calcium from bones also occurs, mostly in the legs.

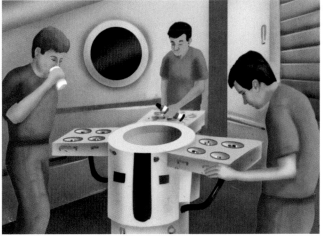

COLONIES IN SPACE

In the future, humans may attempt to build colonies like those illustrated *(above)* on the Moon and the planet Mars. To make colonization possible, systems first need to be developed to produce air and water and to use solar energy or the materials existing on these bodies.

Navigation by Satellite

Sailors of the past were able to map entire coastlines, but they never sailed far out to sea for fear of getting lost. Later, the invention of navigational instruments, such as the quadrant, astrolabe, and sextant, made it possible for sailors to calculate latitude and longitude. Navigational accuracy improved even more when a precise clock was invented. Today, it would be difficult for a ship to get lost, because it can be guided to its destination by satellites that orbit Earth. These satellites send radio signals to ships and receiving stations. Ships can receive the information needed to calculate their exact position at any moment.

FIRST COMPASS

The Chinese began using the magnetic compass for navigation around the year 1119. It was a very useful instrument for sailors because, with it, they could navigate across the oceans, instead of only following the coast.

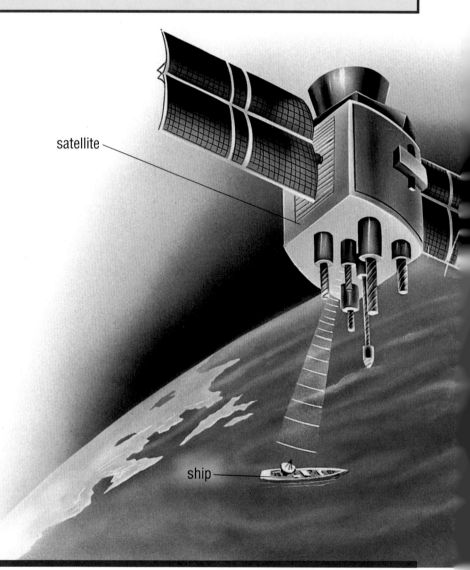

satellite

ship

HOW DID A QUADRANT WORK?

Sailors of the past were able to navigate with instruments such as the compass and the quadrant. A quadrant is shown in this illustration. The sailors located the North Star through the eyepiece on one of the quadrant's sides. A weighted thread then pointed out the latitude on the numbered scale engraved on the curved part of the device. Later developments of the astrolabe and the sextant improved the accuracy of navigation. Today, satellites measure locations precisely.

LOCATION BY SATELLITE

Global positioning satellites send signals to ships and airplanes so that they can plan their routes using global coordinates.

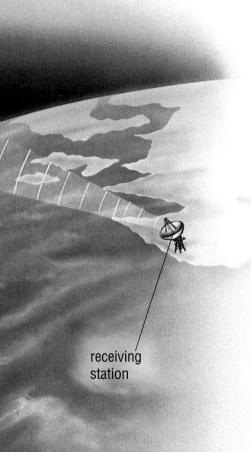

receiving station

DECCA SYSTEM

The DECCA system *(above)* picks up signals transmitted from points on land or from sea buoys. The data is transferred onto a special chart to figure out the ship's exact position. Besides using satellites, many vessels, especially fishing boats, also use built-in DECCA receivers.

The Seismograph

Earthquakes are caused by the movement of rock plates along a fault, or break, in Earth's crust. Earth's surface is broken into several huge, slow-moving sections called tectonic plates. One plate can carry an entire continent or an ocean. Most earthquakes occur in zones near places where these plates meet and push together. When the pressure is great enough, the edges of the plates slip, shaking the ground. Local seismographs calculate the quake's intensity and locate its epicenter. This data is sent to a central seismograph, which processes the data.

An earthquake's intensity is measured on a scale created in 1935 by Charles F. Richter, an American seismologist. A quake of 3 can hardly be felt. One that measures 6 can be very destructive. The Richter scale has no upper limit, but to precisely measure earthquakes over 7, scientists use the moment magnitude scale, a variation of the Richter scale. The biggest earthquake in the United States measured 9.2 and occurred in Alaska in 1964. The most powerful earthquake ever recorded was 9.5. It was off the coast of southern Chile in 1960.

THE FIRST SEISMOGRAPH

The earliest seismograph, different from those of today, was invented in China by Chang Heng more than 1,800 years ago. As shown at right, it was a bronze container with dragons' heads coming out of its sides. Figures of open-mouthed toads surrounded the container. A pendulum inside would swing to make one of the dragons' mouths open whenever there was an earthquake. A ball would fall from that dragon's mouth into the mouth of one of the toads. Each toad was in a position that showed the direction from which the earthquake could be coming.

LOCATING EPICENTERS

Central seismographs process the data sent in by the local seismographs near the earthquake. Using this system, it is possible to calculate the epicenter — the point on Earth's surface above the exact location of the crust movement that caused the quake.

central
seismograph

MOVING PLATES

Earth's crust is like a massive jigsaw puzzle. It is divided into enormous pieces called tectonic plates. This globe *(above)* shows the plates near Australia and southeast Asia.

local
seismograph

earthquake occurs

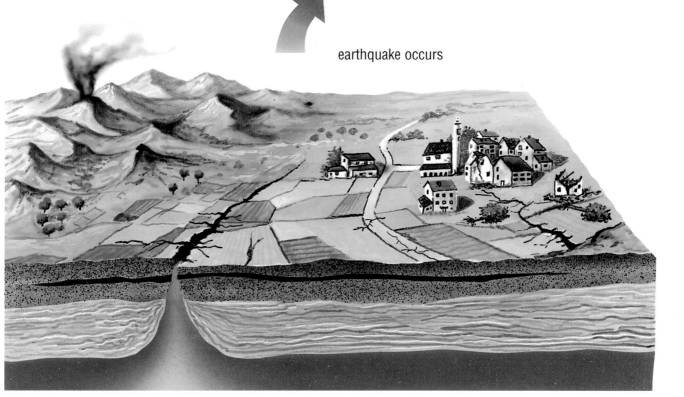

Saturn 5 Rockets

In 1926, Robert Goddard, an American, launched the first liquid fuel rocket. During World War II, the Germans developed a liquid fuel rocket called the V-2. Later, U. S. scientists researched captured V-2s, then developed their own rockets. In 1969, a *Saturn 5* rocket, also used in many later missions, launched astronauts to the Moon. The rocket is fueled by hydrogen and oxygen, both in liquid form. These liquids are injected into a combustion chamber and ignited. Due to the principle of action and reaction, the force of the exhaust speeds the rocket forward. The *Saturn 5* is made up of different stages, as shown below. Each stage detaches from the others when its fuel supply has run out.

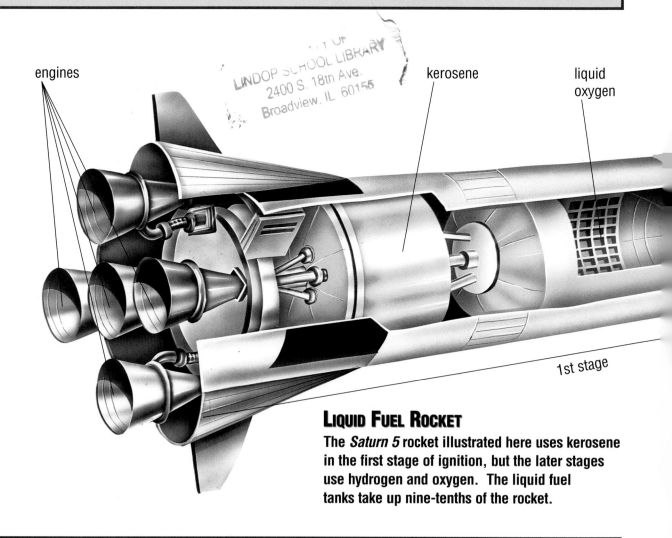

engines

kerosene

liquid oxygen

1st stage

LIQUID FUEL ROCKET

The *Saturn 5* rocket illustrated here uses kerosene in the first stage of ignition, but the later stages use hydrogen and oxygen. The liquid fuel tanks take up nine-tenths of the rocket.

How do rockets work?

Space rockets use either solid or liquid fuels. Rockets such as *Saturn 5*, which uses liquid fuels, work in the following way: Hydrogen and oxygen in liquid form separately enter and mix in the combustion chamber. An electrical discharge ignites the mixture. The burning gases are forced through exhaust nozzles as a continuous stream of particles. This action creates a reaction thrusting the rocket in the opposite direction.

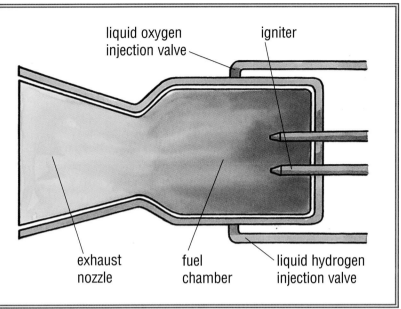

liquid oxygen injection valve — igniter — exhaust nozzle — fuel chamber — liquid hydrogen injection valve

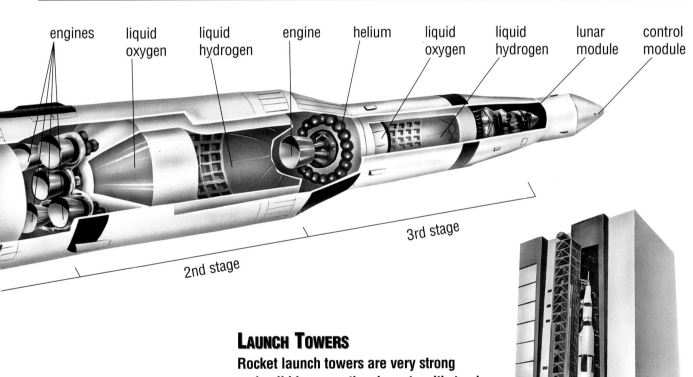

engines — liquid oxygen — liquid hydrogen — engine — helium — liquid oxygen — liquid hydrogen — lunar module — control module

2nd stage — 3rd stage

Launch Towers

Rocket launch towers are very strong and solid because they have to withstand enormous pressure when the rocket takes off. The towers are used for assembling the rocket, for loading the fuel, and for carrying out necessary tests and repairs.

Space Suits

In outer space, there is no atmospheric pressure and no air to breathe. Without atmospheric pressure, small bubbles would appear in our blood, and they would cause our bodies to explode. In addition, in the areas of space that are exposed to the Sun's rays, it is extremely hot, and in the other areas, it is very cold. An unprotected human in space would suffocate and freeze within twenty seconds. The development of space suits allows astronauts to leave their ships and move freely, or "walk," in space, attached by a cord to prevent drifting away in space. These hermetically sealed suits regulate body temperature and air pressure, and supply the air for the astronauts to breathe. Visors on the suits protect the wearers from ultraviolet radiation. A built-in microphone permits them to communicate with either the control center or other astronauts. A backpack provides astronauts wearing the suit with several hours of water and air.

Moon Suit
The astronauts who went to the Moon wore the kind of space suit shown in this illustration (above).

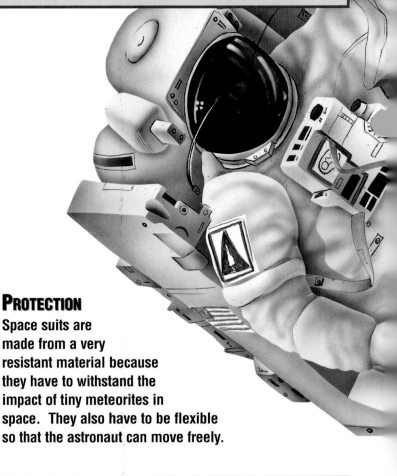

Protection
Space suits are made from a very resistant material because they have to withstand the impact of tiny meteorites in space. They also have to be flexible so that the astronaut can move freely.

GEMINI SPACE WALK

In 1965, a Soviet cosmonaut was the first man to "walk" in space outside of a capsule. Just 77 days later, during the *Gemini 4* mission, Edward H. White became the first American to walk in space. Using a portable thruster, he was the first self-propelled person in space. Space suits make space walks possible. Astronauts are connected to the capsule by a long cable, the umbilical cord *(right)*. Astronauts leave the capsule in order to perform work or make repairs.

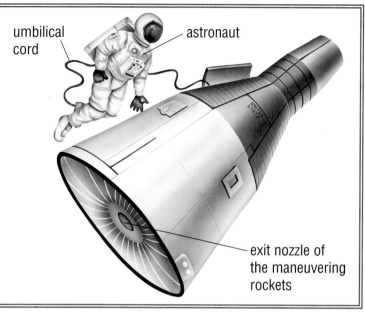

umbilical cord

astronaut

exit nozzle of the maneuvering rockets

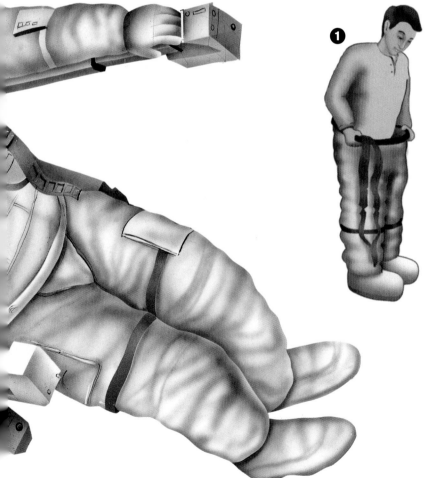

The space suit is made up of two main parts and three smaller ones, connected with airtight seals. First, the astronaut puts on the trousers with attached boots (1). Then she or he gets into the upper part (2), which hangs from a wall. The helmet and two gloves are put on last.

❶

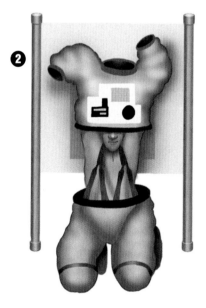

❷

Colonizing the Sea Depths

Humans may be able to build space stations and colonies on the Moon or even on the planet Mars. This would require re-creating Earth's environment in miniature — solving the problems of low gravity, providing breathable air, growing food, supplying water, and providing exercise, recreation, and health facilities. Similar obstacles need to be overcome to colonize the sea floor. Bottom dwellers also need air, food, water, recreation, and health care, plus a source of light. The colony structure must be able to resist the great water pressure at the ocean's floor. Earth's sea floor is five times larger than its dry land, and the sea floor is rich in natural resources, such as minerals and oil. Today, surface oil rigs pump oil from undersea deposits. But, in time, drill rigs may need to be set up on the ocean's bottom. Mining operations could also be built on the sea floor. Crews, based in permanent living quarters on the floor of the ocean, would operate these projects.

DEEP SEA PRESSURE

Deep under the sea, water pressure is very high. Therefore, any colony or base that is set up on the bottom of the sea would need to be built with very strong materials that are able to withstand this immense water pressure. Scientists are currently investigating possibilities. The sea bottom would also become a very attractive tourist destination, and residential zones may even be created. People would be able to spend weekends at these underwater holiday homes, from which they could observe the underwater animals and plants.

SEA FLOOR TRANSPORT

Bathyscaphes, such as the deep-sea submersible *Alvin (right)*, would be needed to link underwater populations with the surface. These vessels could also be used for underwater touring.

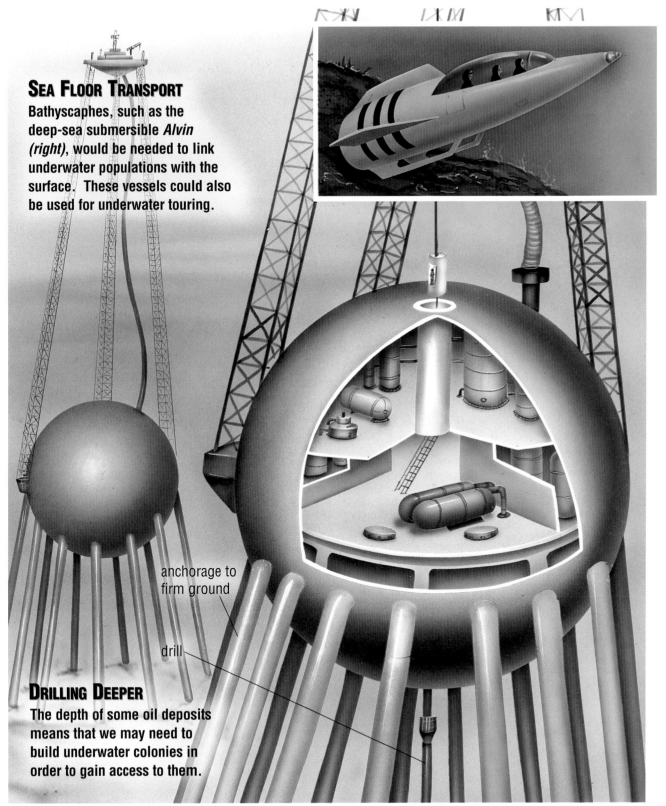

anchorage to firm ground

drill

DRILLING DEEPER

The depth of some oil deposits means that we may need to build underwater colonies in order to gain access to them.

Modern Cartography

Portugal's Prince Henry the Navigator (1394-1460) improved the science of mapmaking and founded a school to teach navigation and accurate mapmaking. He sent out ships to find a sea route to India. These expeditions discovered the islands off Africa, mapped the west African coast, and found a way to sail to India around Africa's southern tip. These voyages stimulated exploration in the fifteenth and early sixteenth centuries, which was when Europeans discovered the New World. Today, aerial photography gives maps greater accuracy. Airplanes take two photographs of a point from slightly different angles. The combined photos show the area's relief. The photos can also come from satellites.

3-D PICTURES

An airplane takes two photographs with an overlap of 60 percent. With two different perspectives, or viewpoints, of the same point, hills and valleys become visible.

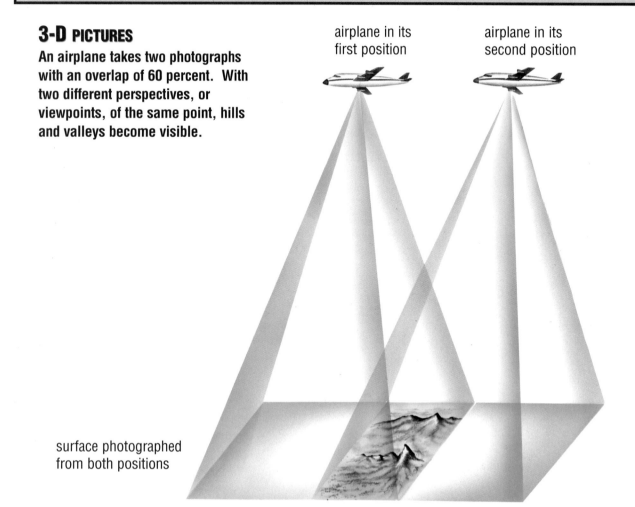

airplane in its first position

airplane in its second position

surface photographed from both positions

EARLY MAP DIRECTIONS

To point out directions, early mapmakers used a "wind rose" on their charts and maps. The wind rose was a circle drawn with points that had lines reaching out in all directions. Mapmakers named the points after the directions from which the winds blew. A map or chart had many wind roses with lines that connected known places, as shown in the illustration *(right)*. When compasses became common, the wind rose was drawn under the needle and was called the compass rose. The circle had thirty-two points named according to the four directions: north, south, east, west, and the points between.

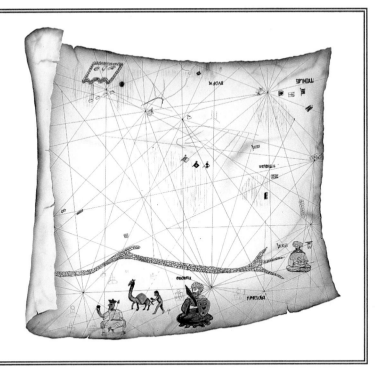

MAPPING LAND AREAS

Theodolites *(left)* are instruments that have a telescopic lens that is used for measuring angles. They are used for mapping small areas of land.

VIEWING RELIEF

The stereoscope *(above)* is used in laboratories to measure the unevenness of the ground. Through this instrument, each eye sees the same section of ground from a different angle, which enables the viewer to see the area's relief, or highs and lows.

The Telescope

The first telescopes were invented in Holland nearly 400 years ago. Galileo heard about them in 1609 and made his own. With telescopes, distant objects appeared sharper and up to 33 times larger than the object viewed with no telescope. Studying the night sky, Galileo made many important discoveries in astronomy. He proved correct the theories of Copernicus, who said Earth was one of many planets orbiting around the Sun. Today, the largest telescopes on Earth are Keck I and Keck II in Hawaii. Both have mirrors 400 inches (10 meters) wide. The Hubble Space Telescope, 380 miles (611 km) above Earth, is the only orbiting telescope. It circles Earth every 96 minutes, traveling at 276 miles (444 km) per minute! Astronauts use a space shuttle to make regular visits to the Hubble. To do some tasks, they must leave their shuttle and "walk" in space.

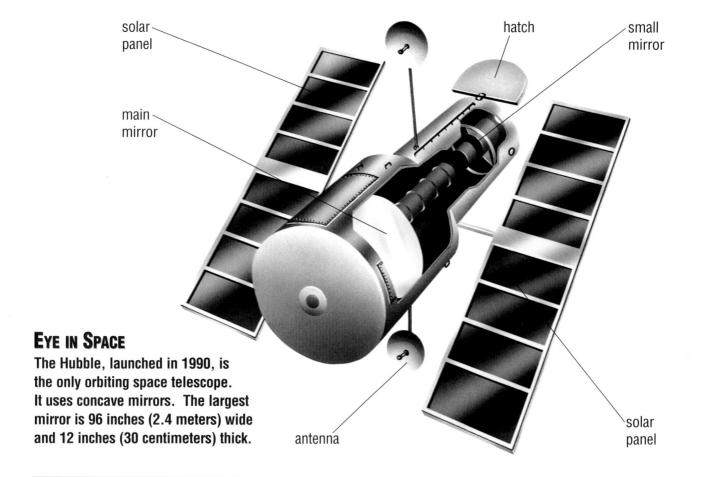

solar panel

hatch

small mirror

main mirror

antenna

solar panel

EYE IN SPACE
The Hubble, launched in 1990, is the only orbiting space telescope. It uses concave mirrors. The largest mirror is 96 inches (2.4 meters) wide and 12 inches (30 centimeters) thick.

How did the first telescopes work?

The telescope that Galileo used was refracting. It had two lenses — a larger objective lens and a smaller ocular lens held near the eye. The light that entered through the objective lens created a reverse image. When the rays passed through the second lens, the light was bent again to magnify the image. Then the magnified object could be studied, but it appeared backward and upside down. These early refractive telescopes produced a slightly blurred image. This was later improved.

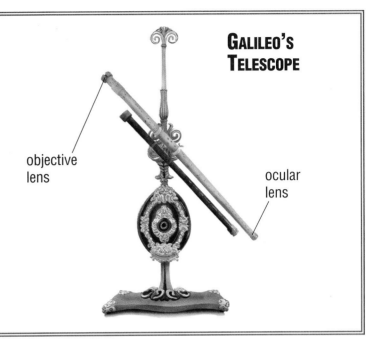

Galileo's Telescope

objective lens

ocular lens

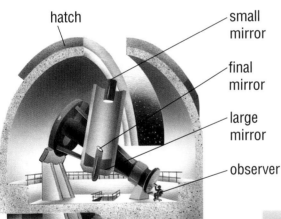

hatch

small mirror

final mirror

large mirror

observer

Radio Telescopes

Radio telescopes *(below)* are made with concave, or inwardly curved, discs. They can pick up signals from space, such as X-ray radiation. A normal telescope that can only detect light is not able to perceive X-rays. Many radio telescopes can be used together as if they were one large radio telescope.

Reflecting Telescopes

Reflecting telescopes *(above)*, which use mirrors, are found in most modern observatories. Large, curved mirrors are easier to make and more accurate in magnifying the image than a large lens is. Two curved mirrors focus light rays onto a final mirror that reflects the rays sideways toward the observer.

Make a Sundial

YOU WILL NEED:

set square

compass

glue

marker
pen

piece
of wood

protractor

cardboard

scissors

People invented the sundial to measure time. Sundials of many styles were used worldwide for hundreds of years. They are still made today, although mostly for decorative uses. You can make your own sundial. When the Sun is shining, this sundial will tell you the correct solar time between six o'clock in the morning and six o'clock at night. This is an easy project, and you don't need many materials to complete it.

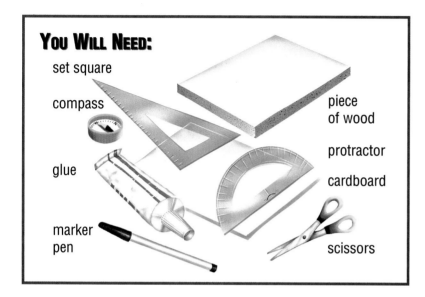

1. Draw a semicircle on the piece of wood, and use the protractor to draw lines at every 15°. Earth turns 360° every day, so each 15° corresponds to the distance that the Sun appears to move across Earth's sky in an hour. Therefore, the lines represent each hour of the clock from six o'clock in the morning to six o'clock in the evening.

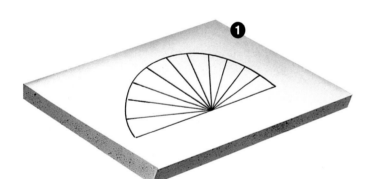

2. Cut a triangular shape out of the piece of cardboard, in such a way that angle **A** is equal to the latitude of your town. Look up your local latitude in an atlas, and measure angle **A** with the protractor.

3. Place the triangle on the wood, with angle **A** touching the center of the semicircle. Now cut the wide end so that it is the same length as the radius, or height, of the semicircle.

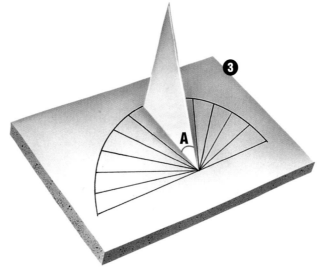

4. Glue the triangle in place. If it doesn't stay up, cut out two small triangles and glue them on either side. Starting at one end of the semicircle, mark the hours from 6 a.m. to 12 p.m. to 6 p.m.

5. Now put the clock in a sunny place. Use the compass to line up the triangle so that angle **A** of the cardboard points to the south and the opposite angle, or the cardboard's wide end, points to the north. The triangle will cast a shadow that points to the correct solar hour. In the southern hemisphere, reverse the direction to which the sundial points.

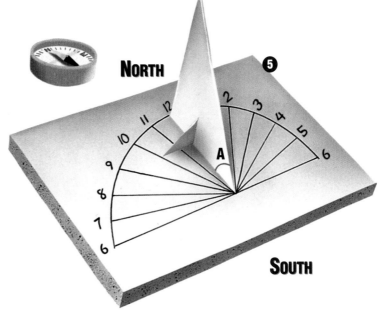

Study the Sun

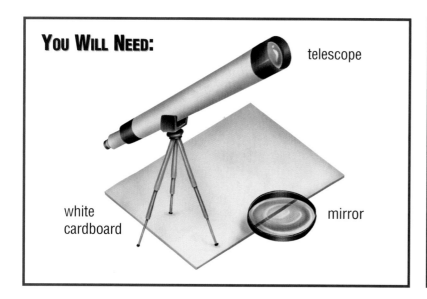

YOU WILL NEED:

telescope

white cardboard

mirror

Scientists have been able to investigate the Sun and the stars using probes that have been launched into space. You can also investigate the Sun from here on Earth. Please be careful, however, and **DO NOT STARE AT THE SUN because this can blind you**. Study the Sun by projecting it onto another surface. This experiment should be carried out in a room that is as dark as possible. Ask an adult to help.

1. Set up the telescope.

2. Do not look directly through the telescope. Instead, put a piece of white cardboard behind the telescope to catch the Sun's image. Better still, build a projection box like the one shown in the drawing. Leave one side of the box open so you can see the image of the Sun and the movement of its sunspots.

3. You can also hold a mirror at an angle to the telescope's eyepiece to reflect the Sun's image onto a wall.

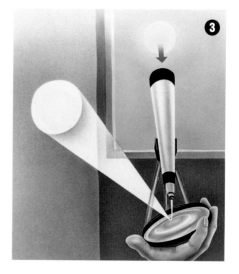

Whichever method you use, you should be able to see the sunspots in the image. Because the Sun is constantly moving in the sky, you will have to keep changing the position of the telescope.

Model an Eclipse

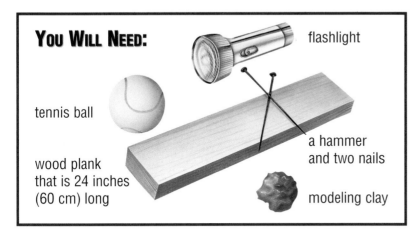

YOU WILL NEED:

flashlight

tennis ball

wood plank that is 24 inches (60 cm) long

a hammer and two nails

modeling clay

In ancient times, eclipses of the Sun and Moon frightened and interested people. Scholars were not able to explain how they happened. Eclipses were understood only when Nicolaus Copernicus formed his theory of a Sun-centered solar system. This easy project demonstrates both solar and lunar eclipses.

1. Carefully nail or glue the tennis ball onto the wood plank. The tennis ball represents Earth.

2. Mold the clay into a ball about 1/2 inch (1 cm) in diameter. Nail it down at the other end of the plank. This represents the Moon.

3. Shine the flashlight, representing the Sun, at the clay ball so that its shadow falls onto the tennis ball. This is how a solar eclipse is produced: the Sun, Moon, and Earth are lined up so that the Moon blocks out the Sun's rays.

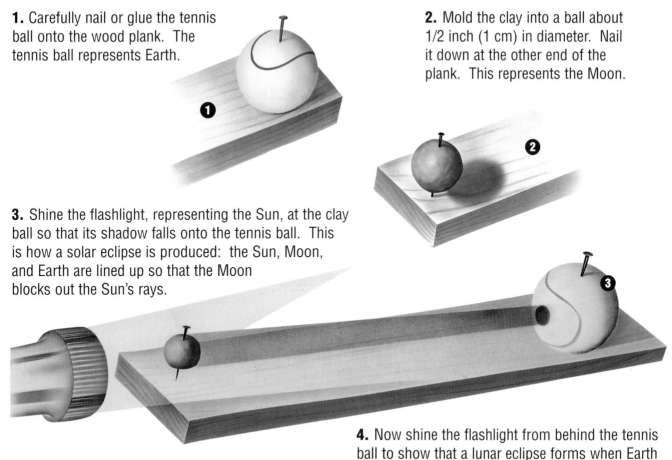

4. Now shine the flashlight from behind the tennis ball to show that a lunar eclipse forms when Earth blocks light from reaching the Moon *(not shown)*.

Make a Bottle Rocket

YOU WILL NEED:

plastic bottle

bicycle pump

glue

corkscrew

cork

pieces of balsa wood and knife

tube that will fit the bike pump (not glass)

When the Chinese first invented rockets, they were intended for use only at festivals. These rockets worked on the same principle of action and reaction that moves the rockets of today. A blast of hot gas moving in one direction results in the rocket's forward movement, or propulsion, in the opposite direction. In this project, a rocket is propelled by the reaction caused when air is pumped into a bottle of water.

1. Use the corkscrew to make a hole in the cork.

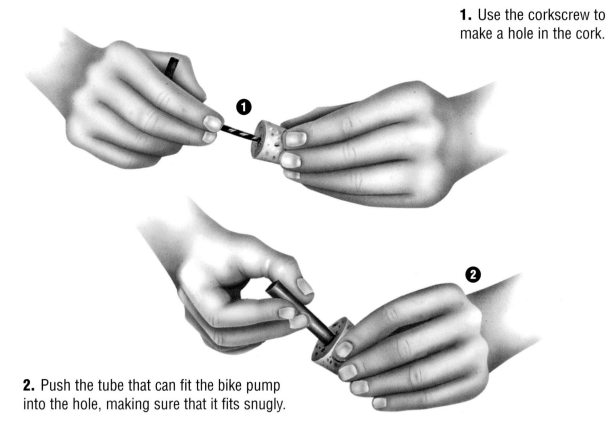

2. Push the tube that can fit the bike pump into the hole, making sure that it fits snugly.

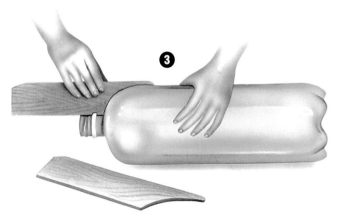

3. Glue the pieces of wood, cut into correctly fitting shapes, onto the bottle to form the rocket's legs. Give them plenty of time to dry completely.

4. Fill the bottle about a quarter full with water, and seal it with the cork. Find a clear open space outdoors, and set the rocket on its legs. Connect the bicycle pump to the tube, and begin pumping air into the bottle. Ask an adult to help you.

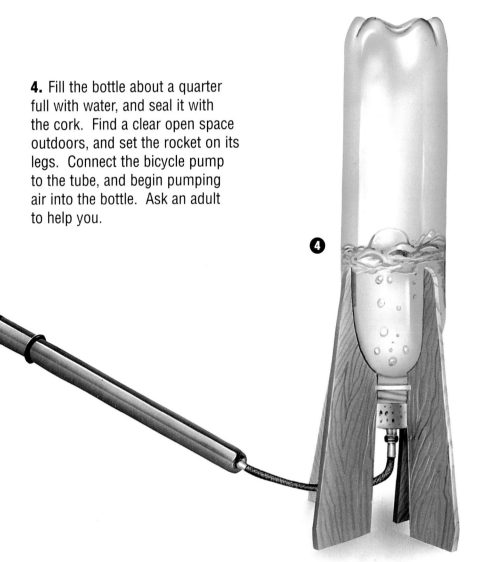

5. Keep pumping until the air pressure inside the bottle increases enough to make the bottle take off like a rocket.

Make a 3-D Relief Map

YOU WILL NEED:

map with contour lines

craft knife

tracing paper

very thick cardboard or 1/8" (3 mm) foamcore board

thin and thick pencils

glue

Here's an activity that will give you a better understanding of mapmaking and map reading. Some maps have contour lines to connect all the points with equal altitudes. Where mountain slopes are steep, the lines are closer together. In flatter areas, they are farther apart. **BE CAREFUL! ASK AN ADULT TO CUT THE CARDBOARD OR FOAM-CORE FOR YOU SO THAT YOU DON'T CUT YOURSELF.**

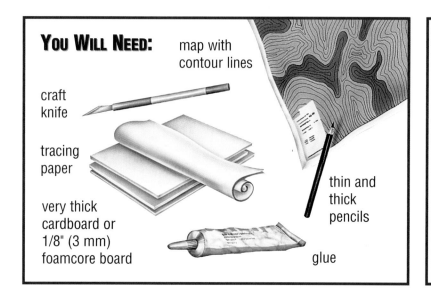

1. Find a hilly area on the map. Put the tracing paper over it and trace the contour lines. Add the numbers telling the height of each line.

2. Turn the paper over and use a thick, dark pencil to draw over all of the lines you have just traced.

3. Turn the paper right side up, and place it on the cardboard or foamcore. Trace the lowest and widest contour line shape onto it.

4. Ask an adult to cut out the shape with the craft knife.

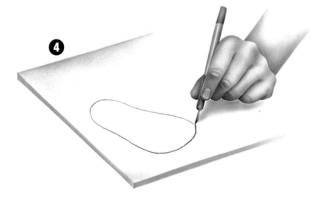

5. Now get another piece of cardboard or foamcore the same size as the whole map you want to reproduce. Glue the cutout onto it in exactly the same position as on the map.

6. Repeat the process with the next highest contour line. Glue that shape on top of the first piece, again making sure it is positioned correctly.

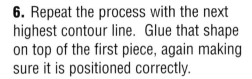

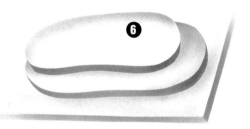

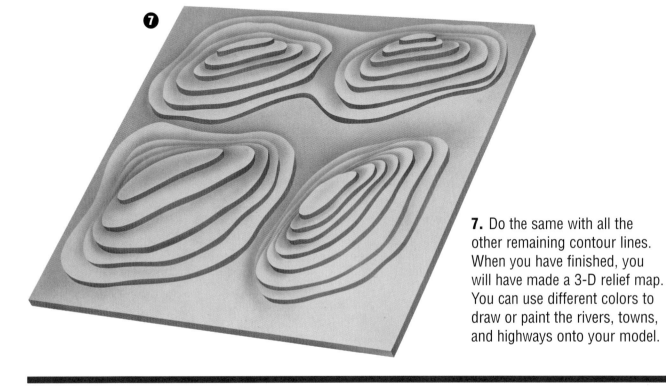

7. Do the same with all the other remaining contour lines. When you have finished, you will have made a 3-D relief map. You can use different colors to draw or paint the rivers, towns, and highways onto your model.

Glossary

astronomy: the science of stars and other celestial bodies in space.

atlas: a collection of geographical maps.

atmospheric pressure: the weight of the air at sea level — 14.7 pounds (6.7 kilograms) per 1 square inch (6.5 sq. cm).

bathyscaphe: an underwater sea vessel, built to withstand high water pressure and used for deep-sea exploration.

calcium: the mineral needed for bones.

cartography: the art and science of mapmaking. Topographical maps are made with lines to join points of equal altitude.

epicenter: the point on Earth's surface that lies directly above the origin of an earthquake. It is here that most of an earthquake's destructive effects occur.

heliocentric: a system having the Sun at the center.

heliograph: a device that measures the number of hours of sunlight each day.

hermetically sealed: airtight and unaffected by outside influences.

latitude: the distance in degrees between any point on Earth and the imaginary line around Earth's center called the equator.

longitude: the distance in degrees between any point and the prime meridian, which is the line of 0° longitude that passes through the Greenwich observatory near London.

navigation: the science of directing ships, aircraft, or spacecraft accurately from point to point.

pendulum: a weight that, when hanging down, swings freely back and forth under the influence of gravity alone.

principle of action and reaction: a law that states that for every action there is an equal and opposing reaction. In rockets, gases from burning fuel move backward, producing a reaction that moves the rocket forward.

quadrant: an early instrument for navigating by measuring a star's altitude.

radiation: the giving off of energy waves.

refracting telescope: a telescope that focuses light mainly through lenses.

Richter scale: a scale for measuring the intensity of, or amount of energy produced by, an earthquake. Each whole number added shows ten times more earthquake intensity.

robotics: the science of mechanical devices that perform operations in seemingly human ways.

satellite: any object that is held in orbit by gravity and circles a body in space. Artificial satellites orbit Earth.

seismograph: an apparatus that measures earthquakes and other vibrations under Earth's surface and above ground.

stereoscope: an optical instrument with two eyepieces that combine the images of two pictures taken from different points of view into a single 3-D image showing depth.

tectonic plates: the huge plates into which Earth's crust is broken. Movements of these plates against one another cause earthquakes. Volcanoes often occur near the borders of tectonic plates.

theodolite: an instrument used by surveyors to measure horizontal and vertical angles. It consists of a telescope with crosswires and scales mounted on a tripod.

zero gravity: the absence of gravity, as in outer space. It causes weightlessness, so that an astronaut floats freely, both inside and outside a spacecraft. The lack of gravity can cause some kinds of illnesses.

More Books to Read

Astronomy. Young Scientist Concepts and Projects (series). Robin Kerrod (Gareth Stevens)

Atlas of Earth. Alexa Stace (Gareth Stevens)

Earth and the Universe. Record Breakers (series). Storm Dunlop (Gareth Stevens)

The Hubble Space Telescope. Paul and Diane Sipiera (Children's Press)

Isaac Asimov's New Library of the Universe (series). Isaac Asimov, Greg Walz-Chojnacki, Frances Reddy (Gareth Stevens)

Plate Tectonics. Science Concepts (series). Alvin Silverstein (Twenty-First Century Books)

Questions and Answers About Weather. M. Jean Craig (Scholastic Trade)

The Story of Maps and Navigation. Anita Ganeri (Oxford University Press, Children's)

The U.S. Space Camp Book of Rockets. Anne Baird (William Morrow Junior)

What's Happening to the Ozone Layer? Ask Isaac Asimov (series). Isaac Asimov (Gareth Stevens)

Videos to Watch

Amazing Hubble Telescope. NASA Space Series. (Wehman Video Distribution)

Drilling a Well. (Gulf Publishing)

Earthquake. (Walt Disney Home Video)

Gravity. (Lucerne Media)

The Great Space Adventure Series (3 vols.). (Aviation Video Library)

Kennedy Space Center: Spaceport USA. (Finley-Holiday Film Corporation)

Maps and Mapmaking. (Films for the Humanities and Sciences)

Web Sites to Visit

www.discovery.com/search/guide/space/
  astronomy.html
www.dustbunny.com/afk/
www.kids.earth.nasa.gov/

www.nurp.noaa.gov/
www.bonus.com/bonus/card/
  Maps_Online.html
www.historychannel.com/ *(keyword: rocket)*

Some web sites stay current longer than others. For further web sites, use your search engines to locate the following topics: *cartography, Copernicus, Galileo, Global Positioning System, observatories, seismology, solar system,* and *space colonization.*

Index

astronomy 4, 20
atmospheric pressure 14

bathyscaphes 17

cartography 18-19, 28-29
colonization
    planets 7
    sea 16-17
compass rose 19
compasses 8, 9, 19, 22, 23
contour lines 28-29
Copernicus, Nicolaus 4,
    20, 25

earthquakes 10, 11
eclipses 25
epicenters 10, 11

Galilei, Galileo 4, 20, 21
Gemini expedition 15
global positioning
    satellites 9
Goddard, Robert 12

heliographs 2-3

Henry the Navigator,
    Prince 18
Hubble Telescope 20

liquid fuel 12, 13

mapmaking 8, 18, 19, 28-29
maps, early 8, 18, 19
maps, relief 18, 28-29
moment magnitude
    scale 10
Moon 4, 7, 12, 14, 16, 25

navigation 8-9, 18

planets 4, 5, 7, 16, 20

quadrants 8, 9

radiation 14, 21
Richter, Charles F. 10
Richter scale 10
robotics 7
rockets 12-13, 15, 26-27

satellites 5, 8, 9, 18

Saturn 5 rockets 12-13
seismographs 10-11
solar system 4, 25
space probes 4-5, 24
space sickness 7
space stations 6-7, 16
space suits 14-15
space walks 14, 15, 20
stars 9, 24
stereoscopes 19
Sun 2, 3, 4, 14, 20, 22,
    24, 25
sundials 2, 3, 22-23
sunspots 24

tectonic plates 10, 11
telescopes 4, 19, 20-21, 24
theodolites 19

V-2 rockets 12
Venera 9 5
Viking 4, 5

water pressure 16
wind roses 19